RELATIONSHIP RESCUE FROM THE BIBLE

What The Bible Says About Relationships

Roshan Cipriani

Other Books By Roshan Cipriani

Rise - Be True To Yourself-Inspire Others To Live
How To Get Through Any Wall In Your Life
Train Up A Child – A Scriptural Guide To Parenting
The Art Of War For Parenting Your Teenage Child- How To Win A War You Didn't Even Know You Were In
The Key To This Life - Conscious Faith In An Unconscious World
Destiny – Past Present Future
The Seven Pillars Of Wisdom –A Sabbath Celebration Guide
Life Lessons Learned
In The Fire – Accessing Miracle Power During A Crisis
The Kingdom Lifestyle - Living By Faith And Not By Sight
God's Secret Wisdom –Principles And Secrets Of The Kingdom Of God
The Greatest Principle - The Kingdom Of God And Biblical Economics
Bricks Without Straw- Spoiling Egypt And Spoiling Babylon; The Mighty Wealth Transfer
When Failure is Not An Option
Real Faith – How To Have It And Why It Matters
The Bibles Healing Promises
I Say What They Said- Miracle Bible Prayers
The Psychology Of Stress-Dismantling The Enemy's Weapon Now
Never Quit-The Secret To Getting Through Any Wall In Your Life
His Poetry Store
The Seventy Two Lunar Sabbaths- Sabbath Observance By The Phases Of The Moon
Metamorphosis-Mirrors Of The Soul, Awakening To The Real You
Waiting In Goshen
None Of These Diseases –Sickness And Genocide In Second Egypt
Patience To Inherit The Promises- How To Stand By Faith Until Manifestation
The Lord Is My Shepherd, I Shall Not Want- Personal Biblical Economics
DIVORCE RECOVERY: How To Live Again
12 Easy Vegetarian Recipes-Healthy And Inexpensive
TRAVEL: How To Behave On An Airplane

Table Of Contents

Introduction

The Bible is a presentation that tells the report of life — and life is made important by relationships.

Rather simply, the Bible is a book about relationships.

Many people view the Bible primarily as a book of great wisdom and understanding. It is that and so much more.

The Bible is a book of covenant (old and new). The Bible speaks of the Ark of the Covenant; the curses, blessings, and promises of the covenant; the blood, people and G-d of the covenant.

Covenant only works where there is character, the sum of one's inner qualities.

Character is the fruit of the spirit.   When my children were little, I instilled in them the idea that their character was the most important thing they would ever own. G-dly character is demonstrated through honesty, self-discipline, perseverance, commitment, goodness, restraint, self- regulation, consideration for and of others, and refinement.

Marriage is one of the covenants made under the jurisdiction of divine law. Men can make and break human covenants, but only G-d has authority over a divine covenants.

We want G-d to join us in marriage, but we want man to separate us. When inconvenience comes into the picture we summon the attorneys. The major problem with that design is that G-d does not acknowledge the actions of an earthly judge who functions in disobedience of sacred authority.

The marriage covenant functions under G-d's authority, not man's. To appreciate the many Biblical laws on marriage and divorce, one must understand that marriage itself was a covenant relationship. The solemn contracts transacted by men and women became their covenant obligations. Faithfulness to those promises conveyed marital blessings. Any violation of this covenant brought a curse.

Another covenant relationship is that of parenting.

The creator best understands the intricacies of his product. Sure He might explain the operations to others, but in the end only the designer really understands how the individual fits into the complete objective.

In order for us to understand the household, we need to go back to the Creator of the family. G-d formed and fashioned both men and women and then ordered them into a separate married community. This is a mandated covenant relationship, structured for the multiplication of the creation.

In the Old Testament, Moses reminds the Israelites of their responsibility to their children and grandchildren.

If children do not obey, they must receive correction. The Bible teaches this should be done by using a rod of correction.

"The rod of correction imparts wisdom, but a child left to himself disgraces his mother"
Proverbs 29:15

"For I have chosen him, so that he will direct his children and his household after him to keep the way of the LORD by doing what is right and just. . ."
Genesis 18:19

"Children are a gift from the Lord; they are a reward from him"
Psalm 127:3

An assortment of human relationships, from profoundly private to distantly national, may be described as covenant relationships. The G-d -Human Covenants contain the same essential characteristics of a strictly human covenant.

Covenant relationships are interpersonal situations demanding trust, responsibilities, and obligations.

All relationships have a widespread application to covenants, from personal friendships to national sovereignty. In the bible a covenant is also the most comprehensive

Covering an individual's relationship to G-d, often by their interaction and behavior with people and His creation.

When Joseph quieted his brothers' anxieties by urging them, "Am I in G-d's place?" he was considering the incidents of his life.

And when he surveyed his life, he saw the absolute predetermination of G-d that was guiding his every step, indeed the very act of his betrayal, and sale into Egyptian slavery. When Joseph considered his life, he saw the flawless discerning design that had advanced him to be prime minister over Egypt.

G-d was in control of his life, down to the most minuscule of aspects. He understood that it's G-d's universe.

No matter what alternate causes he has willed or what freedom he has given us, ultimately G-d is sovereign in a way no person is.

There is no event outside of G-d's sovereignty.

As Job learned, we are given G-d's character and covenants to rest on.

Few things cause more burden in our souls as human beings than when a breach occurs tearing people apart.

Then there are the situations such as Divorce, disintegrated business alliances, parent and child controversies, sibling disagreements and these circumstances are what many of us have handled.

G-d always has the last word on those awkward, conflict filled associations.

This book is about your Biblical responsibilities and your obligations in all these types of relationships.

The peace of G-d , found in His own nature, protects our minds and hearts so that the pressure of demanding relationships will not impose permanent hurt.

We may feel horrible hurt as those we esteem betray us, reject us, insult us , but our relationship with G-d gives us spiritual resources to be able to recover fully.

Each of us needs to learn to build the relationships in our lives that G-d has blessed us with. Those covenant relationships are the relationships that are worth saving.

When wrongs have been done in a relationship and they remain unresolved, you create a ruined relationship.

This book will teach you that G-d's word has the answer for restoring damaged relationships.

Proverbs 4:23 describes the heart as a wellspring.

A wellspring is the source of water for a well or fountain, that which is in steady supply.

The Bible depicts the heart in this way. In this book, you will learn to help yourself as well as other hurting people at the heart level, and be released from the pain of what someone else may have done to you. The biblical promise is for healing that restores lives.

Love heals while fear steals.

In this book my goal is to open the eyes of your understanding, mind and soul to reveal a new approach to living a healthier, balanced lifestyle, through your G-d given relationships.

In a world of confusion, it is our mission to put this NEW knowledge before the people of the world.

Human beings are meant to relate to each other. As humans we are created to nurture love.

The plain truth contained here will offend some, perhaps many, individuals, and that is just the price of exposing long held and cherished lies.

Some readers will be excited and search their scriptures, do research and want to see more; and some will stop reading and refuse to go any further.

Our enemies think we are stupid, not because they are smarter than we are, it is just that they do not understand the power of truth and justice.

They only understand evil and manipulation. Like the wolves that wear sheep's clothing, they appeared to pretend to be for our good and to be harmless, longing to each us about our world and ourselves; but they are dangerous and have continually taught a lie.

However this is their function in the scheme of things, because that is what wolves do. They hunt and kill.

I have found that those who try to prove facts wrong will find that they end up usually proving them to be correct. Often personal acceptance is based on willingness to take responsibility, and recognize obligation.

We need to realize that our first responsibility is to educate ourselves for ourselves.

2Chronicles 7:14

"If my people, which are called by my name, shall humble themselves, and pray, and seek my face, and turn from their wicked ways; then will I hear from heaven, and will forgive their sin, and will heal their land."

Chapter One
What The Scriptures Reveal About Relationships

One of life's most adult defining realizations is when you finally understand you don't have it all figured out, and never will.
It is like running up hill with your arms full.
It's hard to see where you are going , and the more things you're carrying, the harder it becomes.
You realize after several times, of stopping and trying to pick up the dropped things, that you must throw away some of those things you're carrying if you want to make it up the hill.

Life has beginnings and endings; people die and are born.
Relationships are sometimes resurrected, or just cease to be. The more control you try to grasp, the less you have; the more control you surrender to G-d, the more under control your life becomes.
The realization that you are not omnipotent, infallible, omniscient or superhuman removes the fear that if You lose or fail, it will reflect badly on how others see you.

This letting go involves releasing yourself from persons, places or things which have had emotional "ties" to you.
The circumstances may feel permanent, where you are in your life, but it is always a temporary condition.
Life is change.
Our world never considers surrender a good thing, and when it comes to running our life, many people would rather stay in control, even if they are doing a horrible job of it.
In order to be able to submit to someone we must first know that person cares for us and is qualified to be able to help.
One of the reasons that we are often fearful of submitting to someone is that we do not believe that anyone but ourselves will have our best interests at heart.

In order to surrender to G-d, you must destroy all of your fears. When the enemy comes against you, you must stop fighting in your own power.

Fear will make you stop surrendering to G-d, and G-d will not ask you for something He has not given to you already.

In this example of King Ahab, his surrender to G-d was evident in the words he spoke to the enemy.

And Ben-hadad the king of Syria gathered all his host together: and there were thirty and two kings with him, and horses, and chariots: and he went up and besieged Samaria, and warred against it. And he sent messengers to Ahab king of Israel into the city, and said unto him, <u>Thus saith Benhadad, Thy silver and thy gold is mine; thy wives also and thy children, even the goodliest, are mine.</u> And <u>the king of Israel answered and said, My lord, o king, according to thy saying, I am thine and all that I have.</u>

1 Kings 20:1-4

Although he was perceived as weak and cowardly by man, G-d saw his submission to the will of G-d, and honored him.To give yourself up unconditionally to the will of G-d, is not popular. This becomes a whole lot easier when we realize that we have nothing good within ourselves to offer.

The number one condition for obtaining G-d's full blessing is absolute surrender to Him.

The king of Syria thought that King Ahab was surrendering to Syria's military might, and so he became emboldened, in his plans to assault Israel and its' king.

What he didn't know was that the G-d of Israel, answers the prayers which are offered for blessing by this one prerequisite : the willingness to surrender your entire life and everything about it completely into His hands.

The Syrian king was determined to provoke King Ahab to warfare. So that when he sent further, and demanded additionally–"whatsoever is pleasant in thine eyes", he meant to take the sacred scroll.

This is when King Ahab called for a meeting with the elders of Israel, who advised him to refuse acceptance to the wishes of the Syrian King.
As a reward for honoring the sacredness of the word of
G-d, Ahab was allowed to reign for twenty-two additional years.
This was believed to be a reward from the Lord for his defense of the word of G-d, as it is written with a twenty- two letter alphabet; one year for each letter.
However, it was not enough to surrender one time.
The surrendering of one's life is a daily surrender, an ongoing activity.
As history shows, King Ahab did not continue in submitting his life to G-d, and paid the penalty of making decisions in his own wisdom and understanding.

So, how does what happened to an Israelite King, thousands of years ago, affect my relationships with my spouse and children today?

G-d knew all about the King of Syria, and he knew everything about King Ahab and the nation of Israel.
This same G-d knows all about your marriage and your relationship with your parents and your children. He knows all about you. He knows all about your spouse, your friends and siblings.

Just as King Ahab surrendered to G-d's will, and by surrendering was blessed, so also by surrendering you will find your blessings.
Until you learn to relax and trust G-d; to not doubt, but practice what you say you believe, you will never know the true meaning of surrender.
Surrendering your life means following the Lord's lead without knowing where it will take you. It means waiting for G-d's timing without knowing when it will come.

No matter how unique or specific your situation is or how hopeless it may seem, it is not too hopeless for G-d.

Divorce and separation shatter lives. The lives of you, your partner, your children, and your friends and family are all torn apart.

G-d has designed our world so that spiritual principles we need to learn are often mirrored in the physical world around us, if we are willing to see them.

Many people have a locked spirit. A person with a locked spirit has a fortress of resentment and animosity that deceives them.

This also prevents them from receiving any encouraging information or from dealing with reality.

A person with a closed spirit will often claim that they aren't married anymore, in response to problems in their marriage.

And then they just begin to live their life, as though they are single and divorced. Often going as far as calling themselves divorced and referring to their spouse as an ex- spouse.

They cannot hear the Holy Spirit, so they are usually controlled by the demonic forces, and have a habitual habit of lying.

They will pathologically lie, but in their own minds, they convince themselves that it is true. Otherwise it would take away their excuses for their sin, and admitting their sin is terrifying to them.

A child with a locked spirit is usually a victim of childhood abuse. Many times it is discounted as not really abuse , because it was verbal. However to a child, verbal abuse is just as emotionally fragmenting as being physically abused, often it is worse. This kind of abuse leaves marks and scars where no one will ever see them.

That is why it is easy for them to live in bondage for the rest of their lives, leaving a wave of damage and destruction along the path of their relationships. They believe that their spouse is just like the person that hurt them in their childhood and the will repeatedly lash out at them, often without warning or provocation.

Often it is only abuse emotionally, but many children with a locked spirit grow into abusing others physically as well as verbally.

In their mind, they are defending themselves from future abuse.

For both of these types of people manipulation and deceit cause them often to be unable to tell the truth about even the simplest things to anyone.

In order to be set free from this, they must surrender their past and their present to G-d and stop resisting.

Often people with a locked spirit will make threats and try to manipulate their spouse, and children, if they don't get what they want. They may repeatedly threaten to leave and never come back, or threaten to get a divorce in order to get you to meet their demands.

THIS IS A FORM OF SORCERY according to G-d's word.

It is not uncommon for them to use a manipulation tactic called "Control through Seclusion," a milder form is known as the "silent treatment". They will act like you aren't in the home, pretending not to see you or to have any interaction with you or any family member they have deemed needs to be punished. This is how they find purpose. By attempting to control you, their life now has meaning and this means that they are someone very important.

This is completely demonic and is from the spirit of witchcraft.

The Bible states that bitterness locks the heavens, as though they were brass.

It hurts intimacy with G-d, and ultimately with their spouse and even their adult children.

The Bible states that G-d would not forgive those that refuse to forgive others and they would not inherit the Kingdom of G-d.

No amount of marriage or family counseling will affect a "locked spirit" person until they confess their need to G-d for help and submit themselves and their lives completely to G-d.

The commitment you made when you were married, and the commitment you made when you became a parent, was to the Lord, not just your spouse, or your children.

Even if your spouse leaves, and your child rebels you must remain true to the Lord.

Anyone can remain committed to great kids and a wonderful spouse. When you are a parent it is a lifelong assignment, because the only one making people into parents is the Lord.

Chapter Two
Parenting And Biblical Principles

Passing on your wisdom is worth the effort.
Even if your adult children do not follow your counsel exactly, a relationship of trust and respect allows them to draw on your wisdom in unexpected ways.

Ruth and Naomi trusted and respected each other.

"All that you say to me I will do." So she went down to the threshing floor and did according to all that her mother in law instructed.
Ruth 3:5, 6

Children grow into adults in different ways. They do have to learn and find themselves and that sometimes leads to not so good choices. It's a part of growing up. Belittling them for bad choices does no good, but talking as objectively as you can when you aren't steaming mad can help. You love them. You nourished and supported them.
You sent them out into the world.
Now it's time for your children to nourish and support themselves.

This is what is known as conventional wisdom. But is it really wise? Setting boundaries for your adult children is important for your relationship but can be difficult, especially if those adult children are struggling, and they really need help.

Listening is one of the greatest gifts you can give your children when they become adults. Listen to their stories and their troubles, and let your children know you've heard them. Be a good listener. As we listen fully to the person we're helping, he or she feels affirmed and able to share more. Note Solomon's admonition about the importance of carefully listening prior to giving an answer
(Proverbs 18:13).

Then, ask what they plan to do next. Listen without judgment or action.
 The role of parenting is quite varied. In some cultures, children are expected to stay at home with their parents until they get married and nothing is mentioned about them moving out.
The extra help that the adult children and spouses are able to render may involve caring for elderly grandparents who have moved into the family home, or looking after a sick parent.
In such cases, it is necessary for children to stay at home and provide this level of support, as paying for a care giver to come into the home and help out would not prove to be cost effective.
In return, the child maintains their position in the home and may have a reduced or an even nonexistent amount to pay to their parents. This benefits all persons concerned, and is the biblical model.

The scripture doesn't say a parent is no longer a parent because the child is now married. In the same way, it doesn't say a child is no longer the child.
However, the role definitely changes when a child becomes an adult, regardless of whether they are married or not. All adults of regular psychological competence are responsible for themselves. Both child and parent are answerable for their actions.
The issue of whether someone can provide guidance to another when they collapse under stress is an issue of the relationship.

Not all have been privileged to experience a pattern of consistency in parenting, but we all experience the pattern of our spiritual Father, who is totally consistent with us.

The dictionary defines *consistency* as: constant, steady, regular, persistent, unchanging, undeviating, unified.
(Webster's Seventh New Collegiate Dictionary)

That describes the type of parent that anyone would want to have a relationship with, especially when accompanied by a healthy dose of unconditional love and appropriate forgiveness.

One could hardly find two people less likely to be friends. Ruth and Naomi were from different lands. They worshiped different gods. They were separated in age. Yet touched by tragedy and by G-d's grace, they found friendship, restoration, and renewal in each other.

I didn't have to wait for my child to grow up to realize that mothers never stop trying to raise their children no matter how old they get. As our children become adults, we need to learn to be selfless. Sometimes we can be very selfish, especially after our children become married. We want them to spend every holiday with us. When they have children, we want to make sure that we are the favorite grandparents.

Too often we do things to benefit us, instead of considering what's best for our children or our grandchildren.

Naomi was not this way.

She cared for Ruth and Orpah so much that she was willing to suffer her own discomfort that they might have better lives.

It would be to her benefit to have people with her as she makes this long journey home, and as she will have to figure out how to survive without any economic means of support.

However, she doesn't consider her own feelings.

They didn't want to leave her alone to survive by herself. Naomi had probably not only been a mother to them, but also a friend. She cared for them and they knew it.

We need to let our grown children know that we love them and that we are proud of them.

No matter how old they get, our children need to know that we still care for them, and that we are proud of who they have become.

The only way for them to truly know this is for us to say the words.

Naomi had obviously shown her love to her two daughters in law.

Now they returned that love.

Naomi knew when it was time to say no more.

Do we know when it's time to say no more, or do we keep on nagging?

We need to learn constraint.

Our children may indeed be behaving as if they are still ten years old, but we need to show them the respect as if they are a grown adult, which by the way they are.

Sometimes when our grown children are excited about something that's occurring in their lives and are impatient to make it happen, we can come alongside them and help them to learn to wait on the Lord.

There will be times when we will see things in their lives that they cannot see. It's at those times when we can give them wise advice which will help them through those emotional roller coaster times of their lives. However the choice of whether to accept our counsel is theirs alone.

One of the signs of a strong family is how the family unit reacts to stress, tension and crisis as a group.

Being able to connect with each other doesn't just happen it takes effort and building a family culture around getting through things together.

This means that as parents we can set the expectation and model that commitment by being able to face even the toughest times and turn toward our family for solace and stability instead of going outside the family.

Scientists have observed that people with a high level of achievement motivation exhibit certain characteristics. Achievement motivation is the tendency to endeavor for success and to choose goal oriented success or failure activities. Indeed when you set your mind to it and adjust your perspective, G-d has pre destined and called you for a particular purpose. And once He has allowed you to go through the fire to burn off your impurities and at the right season and time according to your measure of faith, the fullness of His vision for your life will show.

Expectations set limits or expand them. What we expect to achieve determines not just what we try to achieve but also what even occurs to us to try to achieve.

Spiritual well-being has been found to correlate positively with a variety of indicators of psychological adjustment and overall wellness. For example, marital contentment physical health, social adaptation, possession of strong survival skills, and resiliency in times of pressure and personal crisis have all been linked to higher levels of spiritual well-being.

However, when we recover a Biblical sense of profession or calling, when we live our lives with an understanding that our lives have purpose and meaning, then the everyday becomes holy.

Many parents have observed that their relationship with their adult child has through spiritual instruction developed into one of positive friendship and admiration.

Parents who have loved, reared, and encouraged their child's development into maturity and a full life of their own, feel a sense of pride and accomplishment as the adult child completes his or her education, establish a life and develop more adult relationships.

By the time a child has reached adulthood, parents have made an immense emotional and financial investment in this person. Scripture does not equate following one's callings with earning a paycheck.

Moreover, completely identifying yourself with your career is dangerous. In fact, the most important things people do in life are usually the things that they are not paid to do.

Partnership encourages dignity and self-worth.

It requires mutual understanding, sharing of concerns, and being in agreement, including agreeing to disagree.

It requires openness to one another's weaknesses and strengths, and toleration. When we can help to foster a real sense of purpose with our adult children it is usually with the voice of encouragement.

Our definition of what is "good" or "bad" in life conforms to our finite vision and limited experience in the here and now.

However, G d's ways are impenetrable, beyond our comprehension.

It is a basic principle of our faith that He always knows what He is doing.

We just have to trust Him.

Why do the G-d-fearing have to suffer? Why us and our children?

Ancient traditional writings tell us that this very question was presented to G-d by Moses, whose prophetic powers are matchless in history.

The text describes that the Almighty answered Moses with the words, "No man can look upon my face and live," also meaning that no human being can understand G-d's just but mysterious governance of the universe.

Ultimately, only G-d, who has the master plan for the destiny of humankind, can answer that question.

We just have to trust Him.

Spirituality is about knowing that each person is more than just their physical and intellectual self, that each person has a spirit or soul.

Spirituality is how we personally relate to our own spirit, connect with the spirits of the people around us, connect with nature, and, in particular, our relationship with G-d.

Peace is positive assurance that G-d is still in control in the midst of all life's changes.

Strength is the ability to endure a hard situation and come out of it stronger than you were before. Both characteristics assume struggle and care.

Most parents are thrilled with their adult children.

They can finally be friends instead of disciplinarians, chaperons, and teachers. However it has never been easy.

The Bible speaks of Sarah's frustration with her step-son Ishmael and Isaac's apprehension over his son Esau's marriage out of the faith.

Most parents care about their children, want the best for them, and have wisdom to share with them.

Children, in their quest for independence, often do not listen.

This is because when you become an adult the one thing that no one actually tells you is that you are now the "parent" for yourself.

When you become an adult you are the one who will have to make yourself do the things that you do not want to do.

This is so you can be everything that you came here to be. No one tells you that you will never feel like it either.

Your parents had to make you do the things that you have never wanted to do. You have to force yourself to let go of your auto pilot, in order to achieve something different from the norm. Anything that will be different from the routine will be meet by resistance. The resistance will come from you. You will have to learn to get past your feelings, to get to what you want.

As parents of adult children, you will have to stand back and watch as they struggle to get out of their comfort zone.

The mind can process a look in 33 milliseconds, if the thought comes and you don't respond in 5 seconds, fear will kill the action required to see goals manifested.

You have to communicate to your child that you will do anything that they require to help them to get out of the fear and transition into their adult responsibilities.
And the first duty they have is to parent now.

No one ever feels like making changes necessary to see even their cherished dreams become a reality. No one wants to feel uncomfortable, or hungry, or afraid. Yet sometimes these are the same feelings and sensations that will have to be dealt with in order to get to your destined life and purpose.

The beautiful things about watching your adult child grow beyond your words as the parent, is watching them transition into being responsible for themselves. You can express your admiration, give encouragement and offer advice, knowing that they are now understanding how hard the role of parenting was for you. This is why forming a spiritual relationship with your children is paramount to setting adequate boundaries as adults.

Chapter Three
Obligations And Responsibilities

The testimony from the past serves to remind us that the same God Who Promised Abraham that He would make him a father of a great multitude which He did has Promised us, "Call unto Me, and I will answer thee, and shew thee great and mighty things, which thou knowest not"
(Jeremiah 33:3).
May we be like Abraham in rising to the challenge.
To often when we are faced with the problems inherent in a secular humanist society in regards to our children, we forget the many promises contained in the Bible that belong to us.
You may have heard it said there are three kinds of people: Those who have been through trials, those who are going through trials, and those who are going to go through trials.
Throughout the Bible we are told of the trials and tribulations to come. We live in a fallen world and none of us are exempt.

The Bible is replete with instructions and exhortations about coming out of sin. Equally important, however, is the concept of avoiding sin in the first place. The story of Joshua and Jericho is another vivid example.
The story of the fall of that ancient city took place during the season of the Passover and Days of Unleavened Bread that marked the beginning of the Israelites= inheritance of the Promised Land after coming out of sin.
After wandering 40 years in the wilderness, the unfaithful and rebellious first generation of Israelites had died off. Moses also died, and G-d had named Joshua as his successor. G-d then allowed the second generation to enter Canaan and form the beginnings of the Kingdom of Israel.

Look at verse 1. "Now Jericho was tightly shut up because of the Israelites. No one went out and no one came in."

At that time it was impossible for the Israelite army to destroy the Jericho Fortress. The Jericho Fortress was located to the west of the Israelite camp, between the desert and the Promised Land.

One's entire life is like this war and one's daily life is like their battle. The key point to win the spiritual battle is to follow G-d's direction. God shows the way to win.

Our spiritual battles must be fought in G-d's way. They had to move forward and silence was their prayer.

The army of Israel's obedience was to their commander and in controlling their mouths. This is another way we see that they had already won the war.

However, on the seventh day they got up very early and they circled the city seven times. What did Joshua and his army do after they circled around on the seventh day seven times?

"When the trumpets sounded, the people shouted, and at the sound of the trumpet, when the people gave a loud shout, the wall collapsed; so every man charged straight in, and they took the city."

G-d brought victory to Joshua and the people of Israel. Finally the Jericho fortress had completely collapsed to the ground. The soldiers of Israel were empowered by the Spirit of G-d, and He gave them the city.

Obedience comes from faith in G-d. Their obedience brought a great victory to them.

Joshua 6 is a powerful chapter in the Bible that tells of an almost impossible situation. The Israelites had just completed their 40 year wandering in the desert. They were now ready to enter into the land that God had promised them.

However, they faced an obstacle B the city of Jericho, considered an invincible fortress.

At some points along its defense perimeter, the walls were 25 feet tall and 20 feet thick. To the Israelites, the taking of Jericho must have seemed like an impossible task.

The Canaanites who inhabited Jericho could stand on the wall , and look down on everyone, and they believed they were invincible.

In the physical realm things looked bad.

"Jericho" can also be something in our lives that appears to be unconquerable.

What is your "Jericho"? A marriage that is in trouble? An addiction to drugs, alcohol, pornography or some other vice? A debt that seems almost impossible to be free of?

A prodigal son or daughter who you miss so much only it seems there is no possibility of repentance and reconciliation? Is your "Jericho" the situation in which you live?

You know that to Joshua, marching around the city and then blowing a horn seemed a little simplistic when compared to the Jericho fortress.

It is only when you are willing to trust him with your weaknesses that he can make you strong in his power. The struggles of this world may make you tired, but they are no match for the promises of G-d.

Not only must you search the Scriptures to find out what has been promised to you, but you need to also meditate on those same promises, to turn them over and over in your mind, and cry out the Lord for spiritual understanding and the application of them to your "Jericho".

Then the LORD said to Gideon, "By the three hundred men who lapped I will save you, and deliver the Midianites into your hand. Let all the other people go, every man to his place."
Judges 7:7

When Gideon defeated the Midianites, he used 300 trumpets in conjunction with a similar number of pitchers and lamps.
(Judges 7:22).
His trumpet message signaled to the enemy that a vast host was charging down on them, setting them into confusion.
The enemy did not know that it was just three hundred men blowing trumpets.
Gideon's strategy came from the Angel of the Lord's instructions.
Gideon was in a place of desperation, as was all of Israel.

In the natural, he was by no means the "mighty man of valor" the angel said he was. In fact, when the angel came he was busy threshing wheat to hide from the Midianites. Basically, he was storing food out of fear and defeat.
In response to the Angel of the Lord appearing under a tree and declaring, "The Lord is with you, you mighty man of valor," Gideon immediately questioned if G-d actually was with His people because things appeared so hopeless.

There are only two paths we can choose. One path is to overcome our "Jericho" and destroy our "Midianites" by trusting the Lord and doing it His way.
The other is to take the path of being unprepared and trying to change things in your own strength. Usually that leads to frustration and alienation of your loved ones.
Deliverance will involve prayer and declarations of the Word of God in boldness.
However, if we will not do our part, we limit G-d's. Listen to G-d's words before you consult any other. The G-d who spoke to Gideon and to Joshua will speak to you.

Some ideologies teach that man inaugurated his existence at the lowest moral level, and slowly transpired into superior moral levels. What the Bible teaches is the converse ideal.
Man began at the highest level and by means of rebellion to G-d's laws, declined to the base levels that unregenerate man now lives in. Throughout time, nonbelievers have regarded the Bible as mythological.
However archeology has established it as historical. Challengers have attacked its edifying as uncultivated and obsolete, but its moral and legal ideas and lifestyle education have had a positive influence on peoples and histories throughout the world.
It continues to be assaulted by science, psychology, and governmental movements and still remains just as true and appropriate today as it was when it was first recorded.

Scientists don't know why or how it works. But an increasing number of studies suggest what people have known intuitively for thousands of years: studying the Bible and praying does work.
The scientific studies all show how powerful the mind can be and suggest that prayer works.
They demonstrate a principle you may have already discovered for yourself. That is that you can use prayer to create spiritual and material changes in your life and in your relationships.
What you say is vitally important. What you don't say is vitally just as important.
The tongue has the power of life and death, and those who love it will eat its fruit.
Proverbs 18:21

You have been trapped by what you said, ensnared by the words of your mouth.
Proverbs 6:2

A fool's mouth is his undoing, and his lips are a snare to his soul.
Proverbs 18:7

Your mouth has the ability to hold you in bondage. Repeatedly we don't see dramatic evidence that we have released evil in our lives by the power of our words.

Do your words and thoughts help you? God has asked us to monitor our thoughts and our words:
Solomon said to his son:
"For as he thinks in his heart, so is he."
Proverbs 23:7

When you speak G-d's Word over your own life and circumstances things will change for the better, and line up with the Bible.
In doing this you have spoken and released into your own life each and every truth that God has already spoken in regard to you. It is literally like turning on a faucet, and watching the blessings gushing out.
You in praying are able to release the power of Biblical Scripture.
By this spoken form of praying, proclaiming and decreeing in such an audible way, you honor G-d, and His word.

It won't matter what the circumstances look or seem like. Only the promises of G-d on the subject will stand. As your thinking expands, your behavior begins to reflect more and more the truths of G-d found in the Scriptures you have been praying and proclaiming.

Maybe you feel like God doesn't hear your prayers?
Or maybe you don't know what to pray for in certain situations.
Praying the Biblical Scriptures will increase your spiritual progress.
You literally absorb what God says about certain situations, and by praying His Word you will see His effects.

This is because when you pray, you are turning the situation over to G-d. This is your only responsibility and obligation.

You are to take the situation out of your hands, and put it in His hands. You're releasing it to G-d.

When confused about what direction to take on a particular situation, Biblical prayer is the only way to pray.

When in the aspect of relationships it is your responsibility in your own relationship with G-d.

"Your word tells me that if I need wisdom to ask you for it. You promised that you would give it to me."

I found a scripture that says, "If any of you lack wisdom let him ask of God and He will give it to you liberally."

Let the Scriptures become the place you turn to when you don't have the words to express the joy or sorrow of your life.

No longer will the Bible be the book gathering dust on your bookshelf. It will be your sanctuary and encourager, your intelligence and assistance. In searching its pages, you will find quotations for every anxiety, every hurt, every pleasure, and every agony.

"My thoughts and My ways are not like yours. Just as the heavens are higher than the earth, My thoughts and My ways are higher than yours.Rain and snow fall from the sky. But they don't return without watering the earth that produces seeds to plant and grain to eat.That's how it is with My words. They don't return to Me without doing everything I send them to do."

Isaiah 55:8 10

Chapter Four
Our World And It's Story

According to your level of knowledge is your level of responsibility. The mistakes of people in positions of power have huge consequences. According to your level of responsibility is your level of accountability.

The greater you are, the bigger the impact of your decisions, therefore you must be held to an extremely high standard.

G- d determines the nature of His involvement in human affairs and His relationship to mankind based on man's relationship to G-d.

Thus, the degree of Divine Providence in a person's life is dependent on the level of closeness to G- d which that person has established for himself.

The greater our awareness of G-d, the greater our acceptance that everything in the world has a unique purpose and destiny and are under His control.

When we look at our present social environment, we can easily see that our people are not fully aware of what Yahweh has commanded or forbidden, and so do not practice these precepts in their lives. They are unaware that He is angry, and that a judgement is coming.

Almost none of them feels uncomfortable about this situation. Almost no one stops to consider the power of the Most High G-d, and their responsibility toward Him.

Instead, they wonder what other people think about them and imagine of them, and they are most concerned with doing everything they can to court favor for themselves with others.

These individuals live in a system that directs all of their thoughts with acceptance by other human beings. This implanted and very perverted way of reasoning and living leads some people to misuse their material and spiritual assets, even wasting their lives in this preoccupation.

If we want any kind of a decent society for ourselves and our children, we must build one from the ground up. And the necessary first step for doing that is to what the Scriptures say and come out from this Babylon and separate ourselves from its' sickness.
The long-standing strategy of our enemies is to alienate our young people from our beliefs and values. We must not allow them to succeed.
If you need to get your heart torn out of your chest and stomped all over in order for you to comprehend this essential truth, G-d will permit that to happen. Don't you doubt that for one second.
Significant damage has already been done, but that damage can be fixed.
Our children are not so far gone that they cannot be retrieved.
So let us take the very first step.

We need to turn off the televisions.
Television distorts reality and changes meanings. Because we instinctively believe the images on TV, our minds are increasingly influenced with each passing moment. Imagine what this impact is like on our children.
The news broadcasts are owned by vested interests that will not report negatively on themselves. You are watching PROPAGANDA to force you (SUBLIMINALLY) to support Babylon and their policies.
Just stop watching for 1 year. The next time you watch a news broadcast you will recognized the LIES almost instantly.
Your mind will be renewed and your ability to discern truth from error will absolutely astound you.
Remember that television is not a requirement for living.

Another advantage of this move is that you will be able to recognize just how the subtle influence occurs when a person experiences Babylon's ways and words and fails to monitor the attitudes he picks up from watching the television.

What on the surface appears to be two Babylon, is strictly and truly the same Babylon repeating itself: two manifestations of the same Babylon.

There was magic, astrology, sorcery, necromancy, stargazing and monthly prognostication and enchantment, And there was soothsaying all under the profession and claim of science and philosophy, just as it is today.

If the whole world lies in wickedness, what makes you think you are the exception?

Evil is cascading down on our heads so rapidly it boggles the mind. Now it is more vital than ever that we know and anticipate what is to come. There is therefore no more time for the relaxation of lazy people who continue to support this evil system and it's crimes, and yet decry the results when it lands on their own doorstep.

The key to understanding Babylon poison is its pervasiveness.
It is not one thing, but many things: things that systematically replace G-d and his laws in our lives. The Babylonian empire seems to have initiated many things we now feel are necessary in our everyday business of living that are just illusions and are rebellion against G-d's words.
Babylon in the largest sense is the whole world system.
Yet G-d is still in total control of the outcome.

Babylon is all over the world and those of you who have been all over the world and who also know the signs and symbols of Rome/Egypt/Babylon know that this influence is worldwide.

If your desire is to be popular and accepted by the world, and if you seekworldly acceptance through political affiliations and the political "process" or through celebrating the world's holidays you are either unaware that you are believing and celebrating the same things condemned in the Old Testament by the Creator, or you are proud of your affiliation with the Antiquity of such doctrines and practices from ancient Babylon.

Compared to previous Babylons, the major difference in what we now face in modern Babylon lies in the intensity, availability, and receptivity of its communication. As far as we know, mankind has never before been confronted by these twisted, persuasive, demonic powers as he is today.

The visible and audible influence of radio, music, movies, television, and the Internet, in addition to the entrenched systems of thought and standards of conduct are everywhere.

This deception and its resulting behaviors have been communicated to us through the culture we were born into. The culture, the world around us, is the medium of this corrupting communication and lifestyle.

We must never underestimate Satan's power for deceiving. Freedom and power will never come through education. Worldly wisdom is the spirit dominating the masses at the end of this age.

Satan's strategy is to relax people into ignorance. The symbols of ancient Babylon and Old Egypt are everywhere in America, and it is not by accident or coincidence.

The Scriptures are our only true source of instruction on how to be wise in these fantastic times. This is the real message of the scriptures.

There is no doubt that there will be tremendous amount of people who do not understand these things and never will.

However, the soul which lives in your body with its Heavenly holder which is still with it, was with the Father before the world was framed. This Spirit within you is two or three million years old, perhaps even more. Since the Bible states that our Soul being was resident in the Spirit with G-d, and is now resident in the flesh, living from before in the ancient times past.

If we could remember all the things which we have known, all the things witnessed, experienced, heard, and all the spiritual wisdom G-d placed in our minds, we would know exactly who and what we are, and no one would have to be taught this.
In the book of Ecclesiastes scripture states that the people already considered "dead," when they die know nothing at all.
But those of us who are "the living," when they die will return to G-d.
So from the word of G-d we know who the living are.

So when G-d says "I gave them Eternal Life, and they never perish," it is past tense. This is why Jesus Christ told the scribes and the Pharisees, "Ye believe not because you are not my sheep."

Then He narrates the parable of the goat people, and the sheep people, because there is a great difference between sheep and goats. Our G-d has always separated the people of the world.
This is once again G-d letting us know that we are the sheep, and Jesus Christ showed that He identifies with His own family, because He is the "Good Shepard" for His own nation and people.
These other nations did not come from heaven, and will not be going to heaven.
They never came down out of the heavens from G-d. They were created here on earth. They did not come out of the celestial and glory regions, and were never in the Pleaides, and star systems moving in the spirit of G-d.

They were created creatures of the earth, yet they do not have a spirit. This is why Jesus Christ did not die for them.

He prayed only for those the Father had given Him, not for the "world".

JOHN 17:9, 14, 20,24

9 I pray for them: <u>I pray not for the world, but for them which thou hast given me; for they are thine.</u> *14 I have given them thy word; and the world hath hated them, because they are not of the world, even as I am not of the world.*

20 Neither pray I for these alone, <u>but for them also which shall believe on me through their word;</u> *24 Father, I will that they also, whom thou hast given me, be with me where I am; that they may behold my glory, which thou hast given me:* <u>for thou lovedst me before the foundation of the world.</u>

Is it conceivable that Jesus Christ would refuse to pray for any people he intended to die for?

No man ascends into the heavens except they who came out of it. Those are the spiritual born of G-d.

The whole world waits for this manifestation of the sons of G-d, and we are about to be restored, delivered and revealed. Having been begotten by the Spirit, by incorruptible seed you were born from above and cannot be defeated.

Having been produced from Adam after the flesh we are born into the earth, so we are twice born children of the Most High G-d.

It is a Biblical fact that the spiritually begotten seed has only proceeded down out of the heavens into the earth by the seed line of Adam.

James 1:17-18

17Every good gift and every perfect gift is from above, and cometh down from the Father of lights, with whom is no variableness, neither shadow of turning.<u>18 Of his own will begat he us with the word of truth, that we should be a kind of firstfruits of his creatures.</u>

There isn't even the slightest chance that His design will change or any chance of anything upsetting the balance of His Universe.

At this time on the eve of our restoration, there is nothing more important for you to know than that you are a son or a daughter of the Most High G-d, and have been set apart.
This is the ultimate relationship.